IN TIME LIKE AIR

BOOKS BY MAY SARTON

Poetry

ENCOUNTER IN APRIL
INNER LANDSCAPE
THE LION AND THE ROSE
THE LAND OF SILENCE
IN TIME LIKE AIR

Novels

THE SINGLE HOUND
THE BRIDGE OF YEARS
SHADOW OF A MAN
A SHOWER OF SUMMER DAYS
FAITHFUL ARE THE WOUNDS
THE FUR PERSON
THE BIRTH OF A GRANDFATHER

IN TIME LIKE AIR

POEMS BY MAY SARTON

Rinehart & Company, Inc.

New York   Toronto

Thanks are due to the editors of the following magazines
for permission to reprint:

"After Four Years," "A Pair of Hands," "Spring Day": *The Atlantic Monthly*

"To the North," "The Furies," "Nativity": *Audience*

"The Metaphysical Garden": *Botteghe Oscure*

"Sun Boat," "At Muzot," "The Fall," "Ceremony": *The Colorado Quarterly*

"Lifting Stone," "Annunciation," "Reflections in a Double Mirror":
The Cornhill, London

"All Souls," "My Father's Death": *Harper's*

"The Frog," "The Phoenix": *The Hudson Review*

"A Celebration": *Isis*

"Lady with a Falcon," "The Return," "Somersault": *The Lyric*

"Song," "Binding The Dragon": *The Nation*

"Dialogue," "Lament for Toby," "Green Song," "Mediterranean,"
"In Time Like Air": *The New Yorker*

"Where Dream Begins," "The Fall": *The Poet*, Glasgow

"The Action of the Beautiful": *Voices*

"Islands and Wells" first appeared in *The Leaves of the Tree*,
a Cornell College Chapbook, 1950

"Fore Thought," *The Berkeley Review*

"Nativity," *New American Poems, II*

The translations of Francis Jammes and Odilon-Jean Périer
appeared in *The Pennsylvania Literary Review*; and of
Pierre Seghers and Robert Sabatier in *New World Writing, 10.*
Many of these poems were written on a Guggenheim Fellowship.

Published simultaneously in Canada by
Clarke, Irwin & Company, Ltd., Toronto

In Memoriam

GEORGE SARTON

A CELEBRATION

I never saw my father old;
I never saw my father cold.
His stride, staccato, vital,
His talk struck from pure metal
Simple as gold, and all his learning
Only to light a passion's burning.
So, beaming like a lesser god,
He bounced upon the earth he trod,
And people marvelled on the street
At this stout man's impetuous feet.

Loved donkeys, children, awkward ducks,
Loved to retell old simple jokes;
Lived in a world of innocence
Where loneliness could be intense;
Wrote letters until very late,
Found comfort in an orange cat—
Rufus and George exchanged no word,
But while George worked his Rufus purred—
And neighbors looked up at his light
Warmed by the scholar working late.

I never saw my father passive;
He was electrically massive.
He never hurried, so he said,
And yet a fire burned in his head;
He worked as poets work, for love,
And gathered in a world alive,
While black and white above his door
Spoke Mystery, the avatar—
An Arabic inscription flowed
Like singing: "In the name of God."

And when he died, he died so swift
His death was like a final gift.
He went out when the tide was full,
Still undiminished, bountiful;
The scholar and the gentle soul,
The passion and the life were whole.
And now death's wake is only praise,
As when a neighbor writes and says:
"I did not know your father, but
His light was there. I miss the light."

CONTENTS

IV

Translations from the French

I

ISLANDS AND WELLS

In the private hour of night,
There are islands of light:
There is one, there is one
Ill in a great bed alone
Who without moving, moves
Like a delicate wind of caring
Over the earth, showering her loves
As a tree the leaves it has shed,
As a ship, world-faring,
Though anchored fast in her island-bed.

In the dry hour of the heart,
There are still wells in the desert:
There is one, there is one
To whom I once came down
From terrible Los Alamos of the bomb.
She opened wide the door.
She made me loving welcome,
And as we watched the setting sun, she spoke
Of suffering Europe, Asia. The world was near.
O human eyes! O deep imploring look!

In the dark night of the sense
When God is only felt as absence,
Prevenient grace is there
To tell us to endure
Since islands of pure light,
Since desert wells exist.
However dark our private night,
However far from Him and how unsure,
There still is human love, moments of trust
That make us suddenly rich, however poor.

DIALOGUE

The teacher of logic said, "Reason."

The poet said, "Passion."

"Without logic, we muddle
And fail," said the teacher
Of reason.

               The poet said, "Fiddle!
What about Nature?"

"Has Nature no plan,
You poor fuddled creature?
You're a rational man,
Not an ape or an angel."

The poet said, "Nonsense!
I'm an angel, an ape,
And a creature of sense,
Not a brain in a box
That a mere jackanapes
With logic unlocks.
I'm total. I'm human.
It's you who are not."

"You sound like a woman."

The poet said, "Rot!
You're just a machine.
You can't write a poem.
You can't make a dream."

But the logical man
Said, "I'll stick to my reason."

(He said it with passion).

THE FURIES

One is large and lazy;
One is old and crazy;
One is young and witty;
One is a great beauty,
But all feed you the wind,
And each of them is blind.

How then to recognize
The hard unseeing eyes,
Or woman tell from ghost?
Human each is, almost—
That wild and glittering light—
Almost, and yet not quite.

Never look straight at one
For then your self is gone.
The empty eyes give back
Your own most bitter lack,
And what they have to tell
Is your most secret Hell:

The old, the sad pursuit
Of the corrupting fruit,
The slightly tainted dish
Of the subconscious wish,
Fame, love, or merely pride
Exacerbate, provide.

Wrap you in glamour cold,
Warm you with fairy gold,
Till you grow fond and lazy,
Witty, perverse, and crazy,
And drink their health in wind,
And call the Furies kind.

THE ACTION OF THE BEAUTIFUL

I move through my world like a stranger
Where multiple images collide and fall,
Fragments of lakes, eyes—or a mirror.
How to include, make peace with them all?

Only your face (is this too illusion?)
So poised between silence and speech
Suggests that at the center of confusion
An inward music is just within reach.

Can so much be spoken by an eyelid,
Or the bent forehead so much light distill?
Here all is secret and yet nothing hid,
That tenderness, those deep reserves of will.

There is no future, past, only pure presence.
The moment of a glance is brimmed so full
It fuses consciousness to a new balance—
This is the action of the beautiful.

Lakes, mirrors, every broken radiance
Shine whole again in your reflective face,
And I, the stranger, centered in your presence,
Come home and walk into the heart of peace.

ON BEING GIVEN TIME

Sometimes it seems to be the inmost land
All children still inhabit when alone.
They play the game of morning without end,
And only lunch can bring them, startled, home
Bearing in triumph a small speckled stone.

Yet even for them, too much dispersal scatters;
What complex form the simplest game may hold!
And all we know of time that really matters
We've learned from moving clouds and waters
Where we see form and motion lightly meld.

Not the fixed rigid object, clock or mind,
But the long ripple that opens out beyond
The duck as he swims down the tranquil pond,
Or when a wandering, falling leaf may find
And follow the formal downpath of the wind.

It is, perhaps, our most complex creation,
A lovely skill we spend a lifetime learning,
Something between the world of pure sensation
And the world of pure thought, a new relation,
As if we held in balance the globe turning.

Even a year's not long, yet moments are.
This moment, yours and mine, and always given,
When the leaf falls, the ripple opens far,
And we go where all animals and children are,
The world is open. Love can breathe again.

THE METAPHYSICAL GARDEN

I

It was late in September when you took me
To that amazing garden, hidden in the city,
Tranquil and complicated as an open hand,
There among green pleasances and descant of fountains,
Through walled paths and dappled loggias
Opening to distant trees,
We went conversing, smoking, often silent,
Our feet cool in sandals, nonchalant as the air.

It was at the end of September, warm for the season.
Nothing had fallen yet to bruise the grass.
Ripeness was all suspended,
The air aromatic and fresh over sun-drenched box.

Critical as Chinese philosophers,
We performed the garden by easy stages:
Should we move toward shade or toward sunlight,
The closed dark pool or the panoplied fountain?
Clearly each path had a metaphysical meaning,
Those rustic steps, that marble balustrade.
It was late in September when time,
Time that is not ours,
Hid itself away.

II

Our first arrival was a square room,
Brilliant parquet of clover
Designed as a stage for the trees
And their subtle conversations,
Diapason of faintly stirring leaves;
The fountains, heard not seen,
Made silence crepitant and watery.
And here it seemed we were part of a discourse
On the ancient themes,
Perspective and enclosure,
Desire raised and fulfilled
To this complex alive composure.
It was there that your voice,
Harsh and aloof,
Mixed with the cry of a bird
As a cardinal flashed through the willow
And suddenly screamed.

We climbed lightly
Through a small steep orchard
To a bastion of branches.
Must we penetrate, force passage
At the top of the hill?
No airy place, no view?

What we found was a grave high room,
Lonely, enclosed in acacias,
Its center a double pool
Where ivy crept and crowded
And water lilies slept, going to seed.
We had not after all expected
A place so perfectly round.
We sat on a stone bench like statues.
Nothing moved.

Nothing moved for a long season.
From high in the sunlight then
A single leaf fell slowly,
And we watched it fall.
So passionate was the place, so still,
This light leaf falling from air to grass
Was monumental. It held
The exact weight of a tremendous word.

IV

How gentle and relieving
Then to emerge, climb down
From that intense enclosure
High on the hill
To the large view we had imagined
Through all the devious paths,
The orchards, loggias,
The long boxed-in perspectives.

Now it was here,
The weight of the trees flung back,
The undulating ample slopes,
The whole shape of the land
Made clear in the golden light.
In the foreground tawny dogwood
Thick with vermilion berries, showed
Brilliantly sharp.
We could read each leaf.

We had to climb down
To get to contemplation
On this scale, large, airy, remote.
We sat on a homely wooden bench
And watched a solitary gardener pass
With his pruning hook.
Indeed it was coming home
To an unbroken sunlit peace of knowing.

LADY WITH A FALCON

Flemish tapestry, 15th century

Gentleness and starvation tame
The falcon to this lady's wrist,
Natural flight hooded from blame
By what ironic fate or twist?

For now the hunched bird's contained flight
Pounces upon her inward air,
To plunder that mysterious night
Of poems blooded as the hare.

Heavy becomes the lady's hand,
And heavy bends the gentle head
Over her hunched and brooding bird
Until it is she who seems hooded.

Lady, your falcon is a peril,
Is starved, is mastered, but not kind.
The bird who sits your hand so gentle,
The captured hunter hunts your mind.

Better to starve the senseless wind
Than wrist a falcon's stop and start:
The bolt of flight you thought to bend
Plummets into your inmost heart.

Strip off kindness,
Strip off shelter,
Stripped down, friendless,
Nor pride, nor warm shoes,
Nor any covering
A cold man might use
When there is no sun,
When heart is gone.

Without coat or cape,
Shoestring or doorlatch,
Or one cosy hope,
Stripped of odds and ends,
Even at last of love,
Where the world ends,
Go rich in poverty,
Go rich in poetry.

This nothingness
Is plenitude,
Honeycomb wilderness
Where the wild hare runs,
Wind in the torn seams,
Where rise buried suns,
Where darkness begins.
Here dream begins.

LAMENT FOR TOBY,
A FRENCH POODLE

The great Toby is dead,
Courteous and discreet,
He of the noble head,
Remote and tragic air,
He of the trim black feet—
He's gone. He is nowhere.

Yet famous in New Hampshire
As one who fought and killed—
Dog-bane and dog-despair——
That prey that all resign,
The terrible and quilled,
Heraldic porcupine.

He will become a legend,
Black coat and royal nature,
So wounded he was blind,
As on a painted shield
Some lost heroic creature
Who fought and would not yield.

If we were brave as he,
Who'd ask to be wise?
We shall remember Toby:
When human courage fails,
Be dogged in just cause
As he before the quills.

II

GREEN SONG

Here where nothing passes,
Where centuries have stayed
Alive under the grasses,
Gently the heart is laid.

Oh, breathe these meadows in
Till you are filled with green,
A drunkard of the scene
Your dreams will wander in.

Then set the eyes to graze,
Set urban eyes to browse
These rich, brief summer days
Among the trees and cows.

And sleep away all care,
Lay rushing time to rest,
And rise up light as air,
Green-fed and meadow-blessed.

THE RETURN

I have come back to these skies,
The clouded, the somber,
Splashing the old gray cities
With purple and amber;
That bloom I remember.

I have come with wild dry eyes
To the rooted ocean
Of wind-wound watery trees,
Every leaf in motion.

I have walked the old roads,
Stone-crossed, uneven,
As the rain came down in floods
And the skies were broken
Like a passion spoken.

I have come back to the wind,
The fertile power
That shadows the bright dry mind
As the cloud a flower.

As the cloud-shadowed petal,
The hooded human spheres
Take darkness and then fill
With a great storm of tears
Gathered over years . . .

Until, so rinsed, so bright,
In the cloud-crowded air,
In my home of gloom and light
Newborn, I stand and stare.

THE FALL

These were her nightly journeys made alone,
The prisoner of seas which cannot drown,
Forced to descend the vertical
Plunges of dream.
Though all day long she knew no fear would come
And freely walked (who once in dreams had flown)
At night, she fell.
Burdens returned to magnetize the bone,
And in her helpless sleep she was hurled down.

Waters were heavy round her; she was bound
To heaviness of falling, falling with no end,
Imprisoned plunge
Sucked by dense air;
Or, worse, vertiginous oceans with no floor.
She fell and must keep falling, nearly drowned,
Yet cling to the lunge,
Gasp for more breath, for falling must extend:
She would be dead if once she touched the ground.

Yet once on that voyage through the night, she was
Given (but how? but why?) the means of choice:
She might choose to ascend
The falling dream,
By some angelic power without a name
Reverse the motion, plunge into upwardness,
Know height without an end,
Density melt to air, silence yield a voice—
Within her fall she felt the pull of Grace.

Through the descending motion a strong thrust
Strengthened her upward against the fluid wall,
So splitting-fierce a tension,
Psychic strain,
She turned weak, dizzy for downwardness again,
But was upheld, drawn upward, upward to free air,
Felt herself all ascension,
And floated through blue spaces over all,
Needing no walls, suspended on pure trust.

And when she came back to cool daylight, found
That she brought with her from that mystic sleep
The saving true event,
The image raised
In glass at a great height where angels blazed,
And there, at Chartres, as the sun made its round,
One crimson angel sent
A bolt down to her human world to keep,
A bolt that struck her knees back to the ground,

A bolt that raised her heart to blazing height
And made the vertical the very thrust of hope,
And found its path at last
(Slow work of Grace)
Into the texture of the nightmare place,
Shot through the falling dream, entered her night,
Lifted her past
The watery dark burdens, the descending slope
Until she was both grounded and in flight.

THE OLIVE GROVE

Here in the olive grove,
Under the cobalt dome,
The ancient spirits move
And light comes home,

And nests in silvery leaves.
It makes each branch a cloud,
And comes and goes, and weaves
Aerial song aloud.

Here every branch is gifted
With spiritual fruit
And every leaf is lifted
To brightness from the root.

Where the terrestrial plane
Meets vision and desire,
The silver and the green
Are strung on a great lyre,

And leafy seraphim
The sun and shade among
Turn each grove to a hymn;
Whole hillsides are in song.

Silvery, shadowy now
The fruit over our head,
Who lie and hardly know
Which is light, which is bread.

MEDITERRANEAN

Here is the ample place,
Hid in the sacred wood,
Where the intense young face
Meets the calm antique god,

Light flowing through the vine
Where air and earth are one;
Here are the sovereign wine,
The dark bread, the gold sun.

Distill all that's concrete
And make of it a prayer:
Air is the fig you eat;
The wine you drink is air.

This is the calm god's will,
And what he knows you know.
Lie under the terraced wall
And let the anguish go.

Let fall the torturing dream
Where the slow oxen move.
All things are what they seem
Here in the sacred grove.

AT MUZOT

In this land, Rilke's country if you will,
Nothing is closed or intact.
The mountains open out an airy world and spill
Height as an ethos. We live in the vertical.
Angels, often invoked, become a fact.

And they have names, Cloud, Stone, Sun, Vine,
But the names are interchangeable.
All meld together in making the same flowing design;
We drink conjunction in the mingled wine.
The journey is infinite and it is immobile.

This is what he found after all the busy wanderings,
This childhood dream of a lonely tower
Set in a mountain-meadow world where the air sings
And the names are interchangeable of cloud and flower.
This is what he found: the grass full of springs.

A sacramental earth; reality both stalked
And made the vision clear.
And here the living waters sprang up where he walked.
It was the clouds and not himself who talked.
Was he the ghost who felt himself so near?

At Muzot he stood at last at the intersection
Of God and self (nothing is closed).
The voice he heard came from dissolving stone.
Even the mountains ascended and were gone,
And he himself stood naked and disclosed.

TO THE NORTH

We have come back to the cold North,
Come home after the passionate going forth,
After the olive groves, the Alpine meadow,
The purple seas under a mountain shadow,
The rich and crumbling ruins in the hills,
Those storms of light in the psychic cathedrals.
After the passionate summer going forth,
We have come back to the cold North.

We have come at the year's turning,
Before the leaves fall, when the leaves are burning,
Before the apples, the late roses fall,
When all is empty and yet bountiful.
We have cried "Beauty, Beauty!" up and down,
But that restless pursuit is overthrown,
And Beauty turned to ashes in the mouth,
Consumed by the consuming South.

Oh splendid was that spendthrift living,
The quick growth in the South, the over-giving,
But ripeness tumbles swiftly into ruin
And death is there under that awful sun,
The fig bursting with sweetness, the grape broken,
And every word too heavy that is spoken—
And we come back now, silenced, to this earth
To bind up selfhood in the North.

AFTER FOUR YEARS

How to lay down her death,
Bring her back living
Into the open heart, the over-grieving,
Bury once and for all the starving breath
And lay down her death?

Not on love's breast
Lay down this heavy prize
And close at last the open, the gray eyes
Of her who in my woe can find no rest—
Not on love's breast.

And not in solitude
Lay the long burden down,
For she is there awake when I'm alone,
Who cannot sleep, yet sorely, sorely would—
Oh, not in solitude!

Now everywhere I'm blind;
On the far journeys
Toward the magical old trees and cities
It's the same rooted sorrow that I find,
And everywhere I'm blind.

Is there a human prayer
That might unknot prolonged
Unnatural grief, grief that has surely wronged
Her very radiant presence in the air,
Is there a human prayer?

It is poor love, I know,
Mother and marvelous friend,
Over that final poverty to bend
And not remember all the rich life too:
It is poor love, I know.

"Rich love, come in,
Come home, my treasure.
All that you were and that no word can measure
Melt itself through me like a healing balm,
Rich love, come home."

And here lay down at last
Her long hard death,
And let her be in joy, be ash, not breath,
And let her gently go into the past,
Dear world, to rest at last.

SOMERSAULT

Not to rebel against what pulls us down,
The private burdens each of us could name
That weigh heavily in the blood and bone
So that we stumble, clumsy half the time
Unable to love well or love at all.
Who knows the full weight that another bears,
What obscure densities sustains alone,
To burst fearfully through what self-locked doors?
So heavy is our walk with what we feel,
And cannot tell, and cannot ever tell.

Oh, to have the lightness, the savoir faire
Of a tightrope walker, his quicksilver tread
As he runs softly over the taut steel thread;
Sharp as a knifeblade cutting walls of air,
He's pitted against weights we cannot see,
All tension balanced, though we see him only
A rapture of grace and skill, focussed and lonely.

Is it a question of discipline or grace?
The steel trap of the will or some slight shift
Within an opened consciousness?
The tightrope walker juggles weights to lift
Himself up on the stress, and airy master
Of his own loss, he springs from heaviness.
But we, stumbling our way, how learn such poise,
The perfect balance of all griefs and joys?
Burdened by love, how learn the light release
That out of stress, can somersault to peace?

THE FROG, THAT NAKED CREATURE

The frog, that naked creature,
Arouses immediate pity;
He does not burst except in fables, but
He looks as if he might,
So violent his anxiety,
So exposed his nature.
His brilliant eyes look wildly out
As if the pulse were leaping from his throat.

We feel his being more, now
We have grown so vulnerable,
Have become so wholly exposed with the years
To primeval powers;
These storms are often terrible,
Followed by sudden snow.
It is alarming to feel the soul
Leap to the surface and find no sheltering wall.

Is this growth, we wonder?
But it makes us tremble
Because we are not able to conceal
The rage, the fear we feel,
Nor able to dissemble
Those claps of thunder
When we are seized and shaken beyond our will
By the secret demon or the secret angel.

To show the very pulse
Of thought alive,
Transparent as the frog whose every mood
Glows through his cold red blood,—
For whom we grieve
Because he has no walls—
Giving up pride, to endure shame and pity,
Is this a valid choice, choice of maturity?

THE PHOENIX

It is time the big bird with the angry neck
We have cajoled and cursed
Went home to die, or whatever he must do
When his heart would burst.

For his wild desire pulses over our heads
And opens the secret night,
Passage of wings that madden without release
When the phoenix is in flight.

Let him go, stretching his long legs, clumsy
On this harsh ground. Let him flee
To the soft black marshes he remembers
Or the gentle mother tree.

Let him go. He has shaken the house at night;
His wings have clouded our dream,
And there is no peace for his lost cry at daybreak
And at night his terrible scream.

He flames through the morning yet he never sings;
He only makes that strange lost cry.
He is angry all the time. Let him find his tree
And make his nest and die.

Though he is God's own angel in disguise,
We cannot bear another angry word,
Nor look into those cold and jewelled eyes,
O pitiless strange bird!

Will he come back, will he come back all shining
From his dark death to bring
The true message, the gentle, that all his torment
Was desperate to sing?

Or—what if it were not he at all, not he
Who must consume himself to be reborn,
But we ourselves who drove an angel from us
Because our hearts were torn?

III

IN TIME LIKE AIR

Consider the mysterious salt:
In water it must disappear.
It has no self. It knows no fault.
Not even sight may apprehend it.
No one may gather it or spend it.
It is dissolved and everywhere.

But out of water into air
It must resolve into a presence,
Precise and tangible and here.
Faultlessly pure, faultlessly white,
It crystallizes in our sight
And has defined itself to essence.

What element dissolves the soul
So it may be both found and lost,
In what suspended as a whole?
What is the element so blest
That there identity can rest
As salt in the clear water cast?

Love in its early transformation,
And only love, may so design it
That the self flows in pure sensation,
Is all dissolved and found at last
Without a future or a past,
And a whole life suspended in it.

The faultless crystal of detachment
Comes after, cannot be created
Without the first intense attachment.
Even the saints achieve this slowly;
For us, more human and less holy,
In time like air is essence stated.

NATIVITY

Piero della Francesca

O cruel cloudless space,
And pale bare ground where the poor infant lies!
Why do we feel restored
As in a sacramental place?
Here Mystery is artifice,
And here a vision of such peace is stored,
Healing flows from it through our eyes.

Comfort and joy are near,
Not as we know them in the usual ways,
Personal and expected,
But utterly distilled and spare
Like a cool breath upon the air.
Emotion, it would seem, has been rejected
For a clear geometric praise.

Even the angels' stance
Is architectural in form:
They tell no story.
We see on each grave countenance,
Withheld as in a formal dance,
The awful joy, the serene glory:
It is the inscape keeps us warm.

Poised as a monument,
Thought rests, and in these balanced spaces
Images meditate;
Whatever Piero meant,
The strange impersonal does not relent:
Here is love, naked, lying in great state
On the bare ground, as in all human faces.

ANNUNCIATION

Here in two ways perspective leads us on
From matter and from moment: we explore
A flight of arches diminished one by one
Above converging lines upon the floor;
They bring us, captivated, to an open door.

From everything that might trouble the mind
This narrowing path is drawn to set us free,
Sends us to Heaven curiously designed—
We cannot help but go there when we see
The hill, the cool blue air, the pointed tree.

The matter and the moment are forgotten
But they are always there, still taking place.
The angel tells of Love to be begotten,
And we, who have been running free in space,
Come back refreshed, to meet it face to face.

SUN BOAT

As if this light boat had no keel,
As if the mast carried no sail,
With no hand on the tiller to guide
The gentle rocking, and the glide,

It swings up floated upon air,
And never changeable wind there,
Only the lightest little motion,
That ripple on the pulse of ocean,

As the sun breathes in stillness, weaves
The warmth in slowly rising waves.
And if the boat seems strangely gifted,
It is that it is being lifted.

The mariner has yielded will
And given to the sun his skill,
And lost his course in summer air
Content to be a passenger.

CEREMONY

Corn Dance, San Felipe Pueblo

After they have danced the passion in,
After the long exchanges between earth and sky,
When the dust turns to mercy and rain,
When the dry fire
Has burned to peace, are any lovers known
To remember this ancient ceremony,
And in the stream of time lay gently down
Magic possession, magic desire
For the river to free?

After they have danced the rain in,
And danced the dry dust down, the crooked wind,
Heartbeat by heartbeat,
After they have borne the green boughs
Many times round and round,
And the drum throbs and the banner trembles and bows,
After they have prayed with their light feet
Rain to the ground,

The tired dancers moved toward the dusk,
The trance of ceremony still upon them,
As if each wore a secret mask,
Though the service is over.
Hunting a human face and hearth,
And changed now that the dance has known them,
They come back into sky and earth,
They walk alone to the quiet river,
With grace still on them.

Each is apart now, bringing
Out from communion, the shared mystery,
Himself alone to the river,
To lay his magic branches down,
Send the green boughs to the unknown sea.
Now all he held so taut is carried on:
He bends to the stream, a free giver,
Setting the magic free.

ALL SOULS

Did someone say that there would be an end,
An end, Oh an end to love and mourning?
Such voices speak when sleep and waking blend,
The cold bleak voices of the early morning
When all the birds are dumb in dark November,
Remember and forget, forget, remember.

After the false night, warm true voices, wake!
Voice of the dead that touches the cold living,
Through the pale sunlight once more gravely speak.
Tell me again while the last leaves are falling:
"Dear child, what has been once so interwoven
Cannot be ravelled, nor the gift ungiven."

Now the dead move through all of us still glowing,
Mother and child, lover and lover mated
Are wound and bound together and enflowing.
What has been plaited cannot be unplaited—
Only the strands grow richer with each loss
And memory makes kings and queens of us.

Darkness to light, light into darkness spin.
When all the birds have flown to some real haven,
We who find shelter in the warmth within,
Listen, and feel new cherished, new-forgiven,
As the lost human voices speak through us and blend
Our complex love, our mourning without end.

LIFTING STONE

a painting by Katharine Sturgis

This is an ancient scene: we stand and stare
As hills are excavated and then lifted;
Swung on the cable's perpendicular,
The load is pivotal to earth and air,
A feather-balance, and so delicate
The stone floats up as if it had no weight.

Below a solitary figure stands
To gentle the long bundle from its bed;
Athens and Troy are leaning from his hands;
The Roman arch, then perilous Chartres ascends
Out of the empty spacious world where he
Nudges rich burdens toward history.

Who with his own machineries of skill
Has not dreamed often of this very place?
Painter and poet lift the buried hill
To build a pyramid or clean bright wall,
And the great spires that sleep in this quarry
Are excavated toward the clouds they marry.

What soars is always buried deep for ages,
Gently explored in the hill's dark mind,
Prized, hewn in slow thoughtful stages,
Then floated on these airy equipages,
Watched by a figure standing there alone
Whose work, humble and hard, is lifting stone.

IV

BINDING THE DRAGON

"The dragon's Proteus. He must be fought,
And fighting dragons is my holy joy,"
The poet says, although he may look caught
And blood is spurting from one eye.

"Sublimate," says the cautious analyst.
The poet answers, "Let him do it first.
Look, I have got this dragon in my fist.
I'll hold him here until he dies of thirst."

But suddenly the dragon flows away.
The dragon is a river: you can't do it,
Hold up a river in your hands all day.
"And what is sublimation?" asks the poet.

"Is it to translate water into fire?
Is it to follow birds along the air?
Is it to be the master of desire,
Or ride a cycle with no handlebar?

Gentle a dragon to lie quiet there,
Beautiful in his power but asleep,
Image of dragon resting on the air?"
The poet asked, and then began to weep.

He did not want the dragon to be caught.
He wanted it alive and in his fist.
For who would kill the god with whom he fought?
And so he wept and cursed the analyst.

SONG

Come let us dance, my love,
Meet in the airy mind
Over water, under fire,
Now every stone must move
And every tree be kind,
The juggler on his wire
Leap with pure lightness
And never fall to yearning;
Come, love, into the brightness,
And farewell gravitation
And now never mourning,
But sweet levitation.

Come let us sleep, my love,
Deep in the dark mind,
Over fire, under stone,
Nor changing moon believe,
Now every dream is kind,
And no one is alone.
You who would forsake me,
Here's an end to hunting,
Sleep, love, in the psyche,
So long and so deep,
There's an end to haunting:
It is myth we keep.

THE FALL

Measure force of tension
By its end,
From the strained suspension
Supported, spanned
On taut skies of will
Slack now, sudden, and
Heavily we fall.

Mortal is the tug
Of gravity,
And the heart-huge hug
That pulls down sky.
Dark clouds enfold us
And then fall away—
Nothing to hold us.

Toward what landing
Do we fast-fall
In this strange unhanding
And release of will,
Heavy bodies now
(Sky, farewell!)
To what earth below?

Toward a new land,
But from where or why
Never understand,
Who you are or I,
What perils and what charms
Come by chance to lie
In each other's arms.

We are suddenly there
In the other place;
After the long war
Discover peace:
I touch your face.

The open palm
Marries your bone,
Beyond all things calm
Finds crucial form,
Lies still as stone.

Flesh is made whole
That held us caught.
There is no wall.
We lie where we fought
Lost in pure thought.

Our truth is here
In this still pond
Where without fear
The soul's alive beyond
What we can understand.

DEFINITION

This fullness that is emptiness,
This hunger that is food;
This union, solitariness,
This wild air, this warm blood;
This poverty, and rich sensation,
This haste, this slow growing,
True marriage, separation,
All-knowing that is not-knowing;
Late fulfillment, early death,
This huge passion, this small breath.

FORE THOUGHT

What is left at the end?
Shape of a mouth or a hand,
Something not understood
That they must understand?
Nothing left at the end,
Not a breath or a touch:
These lovers loved so much
All was consumed. Desire
Burned itself in the fire.
When they arise estranged,
When nothing's left to burn,
And coldness at the bone,
No, they will not return.
They will stand up full-grown,
And love itself be changed
To walk the earth alone.

A PAIR OF HANDS

Indeed I loved these hands and knew them well—
Nervous, expressive, holding a Chinese pink,
A child, a book, always withdrawn and still
As if they had it in their power to think,
Hands that the Flemish masters have explored,
Who gave delicate strength and mystic grace
To contemplative men, to women most adored
As if to give the inmost heart a face—
Indeed I learned to love these secret hands
Before I found them here, open to mine,
And clasped the mystery no one understands,
Read reverence in their five-fold design,
Where animals and children may be healed
And in the slightest gesture Love revealed.

MY FATHER'S DEATH

After the laboring birth, the clean stripped hull
Glides down the ways and is gently set free,
The landlocked, launched; the cramped made bountiful—
Oh, grave great moment when ships take the sea!

Alone now in my life, no longer child,
This hour and its flood of mystery,
Where death and love are wholly reconciled,
Launches the ship of all my history.
Accomplished now is the last struggling birth,
I have slipped out from the embracing shore
Nor look for comfort to maternal earth.
I shall not be a daughter any more,
But through this final parting, all stripped down,
Launched on the tide of love, go out full grown.

THE LIGHT YEARS

Locked to each other's heart, floating at rest,
These lovers stream the night like constellations,
The throat a flaming pillar and the breast
A Milky Way, these shining convocations
In one brief hour reverse the elements,
And bring down to the earth the starry sky;
A single touch haloes the shadowy hands,
And brilliant as the Pleiades they lie,
Floating like milkweed on the winter cold,
Resting as gently on the weightless air;
They will not ever change, will not grow old,
Who have flown out of time and wander there
In radiance that's counted in light-years—
Until dawn tilts earth back: a tree appears.

SPRING DAY

Beautiful is this day that brings us home
From our domain of cold and winter bower,
From iron earth to trees in tasselly flower,
And gentle airs, and the soft-springing loam.

Offhand and royal, we are the carefree lords
Of these sumptuous rooms where light flows green,
These corridors of air, these feathery swards
Under a sky-blue ceiling, high and clean.

We lie on an enormous grassy bed
Sheltered as princes under the mothering air,
Where the anemone shines like a star,
And rivers flow through veined leaves overhead;

And hold each other close in the green chance,
Hold each other against time and waste,
Come home here in a spring that is only once,
And watch how the birds are swift, yet without haste.

At last we inhabit the dream, are really floating
As princes of the hour, while these green palaces
Glide into summer, where we too are going
With all the birds, and leaves, and all the kisses.

BY MOONLIGHT

We are true lovers without hope
Whose hearts are locked to time,
So lie with me on the grassy sward
On the cool black-shadowed slope,
For we'll not sleep in a close warm room:
Whatever we are moving toward
An ample bed's not our reward
Who are mad with the moon.

Wherever passionate love is leading
We'll be discovering alone,
So little hope it can endure,
So wild, so deep, so dark the needing
That even fastened bone to bone,
We'll not have lasting peace, that's sure,
Nor any haven from despair
Who love by light of moon.

So come, though we shall never rest
In any house to call our own,
By any hearth we light and tend,
Lie here upon the cold earth's breast
And lean your length hard on the stone:
Hearts break and they may also mend
But here until the certain end,
Wed me by light of moon.

Now the great open sky is ours
And the long light across the loam,
And we, gigantic hearts of dust,
Lie open like night-blooming flowers.
The homeless moon is our bright home,
And we shine too because we must,
Oh magic that we cannot trust,
The lovely changing moon!

REFLECTIONS IN A
DOUBLE MIRROR

There is anxiety hot in the throat,
The dark wood where even lovers get lost,
The axe held loosely, dangerous in the hand,
That might slip, those cloudy dreams of threat.
There is always ahead some next, more awful test,
Or again the bog, indifference, dragging quicksand;
There is the never-ending battle with
The unforgiven, unforgiving self for truth.
It may all prove untenable for lack of hope,
Something we cannot deal with or escape—

These are the things we lie awake to ponder.

There is in each of us a healing mother;
There is the hand cradling the axe, breaking
Dead wood down, held lightly with clean grace;
There is the help we can give each other,
And every morning, light at our first waking
As if each day a blessing did take place.
Despite all fumbles, bungling, we endure,
Manage to go on building the hard inner core,
A free self that might harbor faithful love.
There is more in us than we have learned to give.

These are the things we lie awake to ponder.

DEATH AND THE LOVERS

For a time it is part of the machinery
Of feeling, one of the several counters
In the game: romantic love encounters
Death and death is romantic scenery,
A stage-device for deepening the view,
Papier-maché of course. It can't be true.

Later it will become the central fact,
Not in imagination's realm at all,
But reckoned with, an implacable fall,
And to be felt under every wish or act—
The kiss straight from the terrible heart
That will not beat forever must, does hurt.

Death becomes real, and love is forced to grow.
These lovers do not turn away to weep,
But hold carefully all they have to keep,
And stare long at all they have to know.
When every gesture is made upon a quicksand
Touch must be absolute and firm the hand.

Not by not seeing, but by seeing through:
With fresh clear eyes they search out each other
As once the infant searched to find the mother
And make a strong one out of a frail two.
These lovers who have learned to reckon death
Are gravely married on the moment's breath.

Translations from the French

ALLUSION TO POETS

Wishing to harvest summer in my house,
I kill a hare and hang it in the cool;
The savor of the season fills it full,
The best of auras, warm scent of the grass.

No doubt this treasure will be plundered soon
And the soft radiant fur hatch out and muster
The angry flies to hang like grapes in cluster—
It is a lesson not to be forgotten.

For, friend, if it's the poets you implore,
They produce dangerous feasts out of their store,
A beauty slowly ripened and distilled.

The sheen upon their words is suffering,
And they are proud of their rich offering,
A poem heavy as a hare fresh-killed.

ODILON-JEAN PÉRIER

GIFTS

I'll put some white narcissus
On my sill, the glass so true
Clear water in it will look blue.

I'll lay upon your throat, as white
And shining as the brook's bright stone,
Holly berries one by one.

I'll lay upon the misery
Of the poor dog, sorry with mange,
Whose spotted eyes always look strange,

The very gentlest of caresses
That he go shivering on his way
A little bit consoled today.

I shall lay my hand in yours
And you'll lead me to the shadow
Where the leaves are falling now,

To the border of the spring
Pitted by the soft rain's stamp
Where the pasture steams with damp.

I'll lay upon the baa-ing lamb
A branch of bitter ivy, seen
As black it is so green.

FRANCIS JAMMES

THIS PEASANT'S SON

We followed his cortege along the hedges,
This peasant's son, he who had never married.

Each Sunday he would leave the little town
To break bread with his family at noon;
He told me he read Virgil then, alone.

Thinking of this my heart swells and is sad;
Death seems to fill the blue sky overhead.

Yes, you read Virgil, friend. For the good rule
Was latin verbs in your sad pious school.

Your father of the earthy hands had kept
Your drawings from those struggling days pinned up
In the small room where the good student slept.
Your mother of the flax-worn hands was proud.
And when the sun was out, or when it snowed,
And when the blue stalks of the wheat were bowed,
Because of you, these two were always glad.

You were not spoiled by complicated books,
But stayed as modest as your village looks
When the smoke rises softly toward God
And oxen stop and bend their tired necks.

Virgil—for me, friend, that is what you were:
Some Sunday evening when a hazel flute
Grieves gently like the falling rain at night—
A beehive. Sheep. A laurel, and beneath
A grave where, with respect, one lays a wreath.

                                    FRANCIS JAMMES

SONNET COMPOSED IN
SOLITARY CONFINEMENT

Drink this cup full of darkness, and then sleep.
We'll lift your pain as if it were a crown
And in death's gardens gently lay it down,
So you, sleep-walker, shivering may slip

Through the grave door where no one living goes
To gather the gold branches of the myrtle
And the anemone whose brightness, mortal,
Will lead you through the young night to disclose

The true life and the absolute achievement.
There dreams are terrible, and sure, and potent.
In that tomorrow's endless blue you'll stand

And see them come toward you, healing three,
And you will recognize them, hand in hand,
Your sisters, Freedom, Love, and Poetry.

JEAN CASSOU

LIFE THAT PASSES

I give to you the ill-provided nights
The fake sleep, castles melted into snow
And all the noises in the street below
My life that passes and thought's raging flights

I give to you the trumpery nights of storm
What's left of them? a few scattered leaves
I give to you the secret wound that grieves
My life that passes, the sickness of the time

I give to you those springs in my head
All the forgotten footsteps, moons and weather
I give to you what once bound us together
My life that passes and holds by a thread

I give to you the binding chains I keep
The silver keys of the awakened prisons
I give to you this time and its derisions
My life that passes, my dreams of escape

And what besides? Then the demons came
I heard laughter below, the thick night's curses
I give to you these maladjusted verses
My life that passes withdrawn in your name

I give to you all that you can't dispel
Sleepwalker that I am, hugging dead skin
Acrobat on a tightrope threaded thin
My life that is lived badly and on will.

PIERRE SEGHERS

THE VOYAGES

When from a cloud a sudden bird bursts free
Pure fools have but to touch it as it flies
And it's time to inhabit space and be
Flown faster than tears fall or than sighs
To where children and Magi have a country.

Brothers, my fingertips salute you, going
Upon that voyage where spring follows you:
One breath, it's earth; one word, it's water flowing,
A murmur, and the night is born anew
As long as your mouth thirsts for the Unknowing.

Those dwellers in the eye and in the ear
Have built them palaces of crystal walls
Guests of the deep woods, of the drowsy mere
Through silent paths and through dark intervals
Bring me your sun, your great burning sphere.

O book open to the pure fool's hand
O book of that hour when love's shining through
I am the child of all that fertile land
Who among flocks of days still waits for you
That body may at last join in the round.

ROBERT SABATIER

JUL 2 7 1999	DATE DUE	
FEB 2 8 2002		

1986

30

1997